Revolt. She said. Revolt again.

Alice Birch has previously worked at the Royal Court on works such as *Peckham: The Soap Opera* and *Revolt. She said. Revolt again.* (RSC). Other credits include: *We Want You To Watch* (National), *The Lone Pine Club* (Pentabus), *Little Light* (Orange Tree), *Little on the Inside* (Almeida / Clean Break), *Salt* (Comedie de Valence), *Many Moons* (Theatre 503), *Flying the Nest* (BBC Radio 4) and *Lady Macbeth* (BBC Films / BFI / Creative England). Alice was the co-winner of the 2014 George Devine Award for *Revolt. She said. Revolt again.* and winner of the Arts Foundation Award for Playwriting 2014.

Dr Marissia Fragkou is assistant professor of theatre at the Aristotle University of Thessaloniki (Greece). Her essays on contemporary British and European theatre have been published in *Modern Drama*, *Didaskalia*, *Performing Ethos*, *Contemporary Theatre Review* and edited volumes by Bloomsbury, Routledge, Palgrave and MUP. She is the author of *Ecologies of Precarity in Twenty-First Century Theatre: Politics, Affect, Responsibility* (Bloomsbury, 2019).

T0282225

Revolt. She said. Revolt again.

ALICE BIRCH

With commentary and notes by

MARISSIA FRAGKOU

Series Editors: Jenny Stevens, Matthew Nichols,
Sara Freeman and Chris Megson

methuen | drama

LONDON · NEW YORK · OXFORD · NEW DELHI · SYDNEY

METHUEN DRAMA
Bloomsbury Publishing Plc
50 Bedford Square, London, WC1B 3DP, UK
1385 Broadway, New York, NY 10018, USA
29 Farlsfort Terrace, Dublin 2, Ireland

BLOOMSBURY, METHUEN DRAMA and the Methuen Drama logo are trademarks
of Bloomsbury Publishing Plc

First published in Great Britain by Oberon Books 2014
This edition published by Methuen Drama 2024

Revolt. She said. Revolt again. © 2014
Commentary and Notes © Marissia Fragkou, 2024

A catalogue record for this book is available from the British Library.

ISBN: PB: 978-1-3502-6440-3
       ePDF: 978-1-3502-6441-0
       eBook: 978-1-3502-6442-7

Series: Student Editions

Typeset by RefineCatch Limited, Bungay, Suffolk
Printed and bound in India

To find out more about our authors and books visit www.bloomsbury.com
and sign up for our newsletters.

Contents

Introduction

Historical and cultural contexts

Revolt. She said. Revolt again. (hereafter *Revolt*) was written in three days in response to the slogan 'Well behaved women seldom make history' put forward by American feminist historian Laurel Thatcher Ulrich in the late 1970s. The play anticipated the reinvigoration of feminism in the second decade of the twenty-first century, which saw feminist books such as Chimamanda Ngozi Adichie's *We Should All Be Feminists* (2014) and Caitlin Moran's *How to Be a Woman* (2014) becoming bestsellers and feminist activism seeking justice for women who experience abuse gaining a global momentum. In 2017, a few years after the play's premiere, #MeToo (founded by Black activist Tarana Burke in 2006) erupted as a global solidarity movement among women after actress and producer Alyssa Milano invited her Twitter followers to share their own stories of sexual harassment. Following suit, other celebrity figures such as Emma Watson and Reese Witherspoon openly spoke about structural inequalities in the entertainment industry and rampant cases of sexual harassment.

This feminist mobilization has taken the form of a critical re-evaluation of the 1970s second-wave feminist movement (Aston, 2021, p. 3). Although a multi-dimensional movement with different strands, second-wave feminism broadly sought to dismantle patriarchal structures and their damaging impact on the experiences of women; questions around sexism, sexual harassment, rape, reproductive rights and equal pay played a crucial role in advancing women's equality and autonomy and laid the foundation for several legal and cultural reforms. The #MeToo generation has also experienced the impact of so-called postfeminism, an ideology that mainly dominated the 1990s and early 2000s, which advocated for individual success and promoted the illusion that the feminist cause has been won. In contrast, twenty-first-century feminisms such as the #MeToo movement highlight the necessity to return to and provoke discussion about issues that continue to damage women's lives, thus striving for a positive change; they have also advanced the theme of intersectionality, first discussed by 1970s Black feminists to index how gender oppression interlaces with race, by examining how patriarchy creates more stratified inequalities in terms of race, class, sexuality, ability and age.

Revolt directly taps into questions concerning gender power structures and the debate against postfeminism, developing a critique against ideas of 'success' and 'choice' as illusionary and accessible only to a minority of women. The play's acute focus on the power of language in maintaining structures of inequality and exclusion further speaks to what is often labelled as 'wokeness culture', a loaded term which refers to a wider and often controversial twenty-first-century movement of critical awareness (particularly among the young generation) regarding the existence of structural inequalities and the need to openly expose them.

Theatrical contexts

The central theme of revolt which dominates the play both in content and form is signalled in the published script as an instruction to the creative team: 'this play should not be well behaved' (p. 7). In addition to challenging forms of power that perpetuate sexism and the commodification of and violence against the female body, *Revolt* revolutionizes dramatic form in order to communicate a profound disaffection with patriarchal structures. This can be seen, for example, in the play's dramaturgical structure comprised by a variety of scenes, each bearing a different title, which altogether compose a revolution manual. Searching for a theatrical form that captures the critique against gender injustices has been a chief concern in feminist theatre and performance work since the 1960s. Whilst citing well-established twentieth-century feminist ideas, *Revolt* also expresses a disappointment with the failure of previous feminisms to overthrow patriarchal and capitalist structures that contribute to the oppression of women and other marginalized identities. In doing so, the play asks what strategies can best achieve gender equality and social justice for the twenty-first century.

A key preoccupation of second-wave feminisms has been to challenge widely held assumptions which associate women with the private sphere and men with the public sphere; this arbitrary division perpetuates the idea that women are owned by men whilst also rendering invisible women's caregiving labour which takes place at home. One of the most famous feminist slogans 'the personal is political' was taken up by twentieth-century feminist theatre makers in order to offer women a public space to reclaim their voice in a patriarchal and male-led industry. Taking into consideration the notable absence of women from the great works of literature and theatre, what scholars refer to as 'the canon', feminist theatre seeks to redress this imbalance by allowing women to represent themselves on stage. This has been pursued through creating more roles for female performers and prioritizing the female voice which has been previously either hidden or male-produced, hence lacking authenticity and concealing the thoughts and desires of 'real' women. Several feminist plays revisited familiar stories and characters from the canon of Shakespeare and the classics in order to examine them through alternative points of view and unearth new histories or silenced 'herstories'.

By allowing women to represent themselves rather than being represented, feminist theatre challenges problematic stereotypes that classify women in specific categories such as, on the one hand, the innocent/virgin/obedient/silent/fragile woman and, on the other, the whore/vamp/transgressive/mad woman by offering more complex representations. Through its focus on specific thematic areas such as language, marriage, work and the body, *Revolt* taps into several central concerns that can be traced back to the legacies of twentieth-century feminist theatre, such as the examination of the institution of marriage, the bond between mothers and daughters, the role of sisterhood and solidarity among women, the possibilities for breaking the glass ceiling in the workplace, the problematic nature of gender stereotypes and the impact of the commodification and sexualization of the female body which aims to satisfy male heterosexual desire.

The use of dramatic devices such as fast-paced dialogue and overlapping speeches which uncover relations of power among the different performers-characters also places emphasis on how the construction of language perpetuates gender hierarchies that favour male perspectives whilst silencing women. In addition, the play's experimentation with non-realist forms further connects *Revolt* with feminist debates concerning language's inherent sexism. Various strands of feminist criticism consider language as a male construct; as a result, women are forced to use a language which fails to capture their identity in order to be able to occupy a place in mainstream culture. Feminist theatre has also been dogged by similar questions over which dramaturgical devices can best represent women's experience without silencing them; it is for this reason that some feminist theatre makers often take issue with realism, comparing it to a '"prisonhouse of art" for women' that entraps them within rigid stereotypes and maintains power structures intact (Case, 2008, p. 124). With its frequent emphasis on closure and linearity, it participates in representing a restricted version of the world that does not necessarily correspond to the experiences of women. Although feminist theatre scholars have recently questioned the claims that compare realism to a 'prisonhouse', this debate still presents a fascinating discussion about the power of language and style in shaping shared beliefs about the female voice, authenticity, gender and visibility and is particularly relevant for this play and its strong experimentation with dramatic language.

Revolt shares allegiance to plays by other women playwrights who sought to invent a dramatic language (in terms of both content and form) that can capture the impact of gender oppression and marginalization on the experiences of women. One such example is Caryl Churchill who has been described by critics as 'the mother of reinvention' for her eclectic experimentation with dramatic form and a playwright committed to socialist feminist ideas (Benedict, 1997, p. 4). Her ground-breaking all-female play *Top Girls* (1982) cautions against the pitfalls of feminist ideas popularized during the 1980s that privileged white middle-class women at the cost of creating solidarity among women from different class, gender and ethnic backgrounds; the play also troubles capitalist ideas of success as an ultimate goal that will win women equality. Similarly, *Revolt* navigates the vicissitudes of postfeminism which presents the false claim that gender equality in the twenty-first century has been achieved. Similar to *Top Girls* where Marlene's teenage daughter Angie represents the uncertain future that young women of her generation will inherit, Act 2 in *Revolt* features Agnes, a young woman who has lost her ability to speak, eat or lift her hands due to the absence of positive role models. A further shared feature between the two plays is the use of overlapping speech, first introduced by Churchill with *Three More Sleepless Nights* (1980) and further explored in *Top Girls*.

Revolt takes issue with the sexualization and commodification of the female body through the media and the pornography industry that subjugate women to the position of objects. In Act 3 in particular, there is reference to the pornographic imagery that degrades women and is connected to wider practices of gender-based violence; this concern strongly echoes Sarah Daniels' play *Masterpieces* (1983), which took a stand against the damaging impact of the pornography industry, thus participating in a heated feminist debate of the time. *Revolt* further places emphasis on the imagery of the vagina, which represents female empowerment and the subjection of the female body to violence; in doing so, it resonates with V Ensler's *The Vagina Monologues* (1996) and its emphasis on the female sexual organ as an instrument of power to challenge patriarchal perspectives. *Revolt* further shares common ground with Black playwright debbie tucker green for her linguistic precision, use of punctuation, and strong commitment to the position of women in precarious social milieus, as well as Sarah Kane for her taboo-breaking imagery and language and bold destruction of realist dramatic structures.

As both text and performance, *Revolt* can be read against feminist performance art and autobiographical performance that explores how 'personal' women's stories become 'political'. Female performance artists from Marina Abramović, Carolee Schneemann, Hannah Wilke, Bobby Baker, Selina Thompson and Ray Young, have placed emphasis on the female body, presenting it in forms that resist characterization and where the *real* physical experience of the performer's body is foregrounded and shared with an audience. In this way, performance art reveals the porous boundaries between art and life or character and actor. *Revolt* indicates that offstage and onstage are continuous, thus laying bare costume and make-up changes and drawing attention to the thin line between actor and character. The stage directions often ask us to consider whether the person who speaks is the character or the actor or whether the actors have forgotten their lines; characters often fail to understand the world around them, imbuing the play with a feeling of uncertainty. Further moments reveal communication failure between characters which often expose language as a construct. The idea of failure that permeates the play in both form and content has become a recurrent theme in contemporary theatre and can be traced back to the work of Samuel Beckett. Rather than stultifying, failure can challenge dominant ideas and create openings for different points of view (Bailes, 2011, p. 2). Failure has also been read as a feminist strategy of resistance against structures of oppression which offers more agency to the performing subject (Gorman, 2021, p. 2).

The above stylistic features that can be seen in *Revolt*, such as failure, the fluidity between actor-character and laying bare the processes of theatre making, also belong to the genre of postdramatic theatre. Postdramatic theatre offers new and playful ways of looking at both text and theatrical event: action and plot resist linearity and closure and there is no focus on a single storyline; there is limited interest in psychologically driven characterization; stagecraft elements such as scenography or music play an equally important role as the spoken text, and the spectator is often made aware that they share the same space and time with the performers on stage.

Scene analysis

Revolt is divided into four acts (although the final act is significantly shorter than the others) and the first three are introduced through short titles in the form of an instruction manual. There is no indication of specific genders although, as the author highlights in her note to the play, 'there should be at least one female character (that should probably be played by a female actor) in every scene' (p. 7). As will be detailed below, each act is written in a different style which creates a narrative that resists the idea of a single voice.

Act 1

Act 1 is divided into four sections each carrying an instruction that begins with the prompt 'Revolutionize'. The main focus is on language, marriage, work and the body, and how these are shaped by gender power relations. Each scene resembles a battle for power and begins with the phrase, 'I don't understand', which is spoken by the character who takes on the role of the person whose authority is challenged.

The first scene, 'Revolutionize the Language. (Invert It.)', stages the conversation of a couple (possibly a male and a female) who are about to engage in sexual intercourse. The whole act of love-making is unfolding on the linguistic realm as its key concern is to humorously expose and challenge language's inherent sexism. From the dialogue, it is clear that the male character begins to make advances towards the other character by expressing his desire: 'You are a Brilliant Bright Bright thing – do you have any idea what your shoulders, bare like that, do to me, do to my structure, to my insides' (p. 9). Later on, the same character continues to narrate how he was fantasizing making love to his partner over dinner; this desire is constantly objectifying the woman's body who tries to resist it by 'inverting' language. She challenges the choice of vocabulary of her interlocutor by proposing minor changes such as, 'I want to make Love *with* you' rather than '*to* you' (p. 12) or refusing to respond to statements such as 'I'm going to peel your dress' (p. 14) or 'spread your legs' (p. 14) or 'baby consume me' (p. 18). At the end of the scene, she slowly reclaims the male's phallic power through her female sex organ which she presents not like a 'gap' but as powerful and strong: 'I am Drowning and Suffocating and Overwhelming you with my Giant Organ' (p. 18).

The second scene, 'Revolutionize the World. (Do not Marry.)', continues to explore the nature of love and commitment between couples, this time focusing on the institution of marriage. The scene begins at the point when one of the characters is responding to a marriage proposal she has just received that has taken her by surprise. The play invokes the patriarchal structures that have historically underpinned marriage and are still percolating today, such as the perception of women as a reproductive vessel without real autonomy over their bodies, and marriage as a financial transaction between men (the husband and the bride's father). We are presented with an explosive metaphor comparing the marriage proposal to an invitation for a suicide bombing attack – where a wedding ring represents a bomb – in order to challenge patriarchal assumptions that all women should get married. Although the (possibly) male character is trying to justify the proposal on the basis of his love and commitment, the more he tries to express his intentions ('I said you are the most important human being to me [. . .] that you you make me laugh more than anyone [. . .]. What I said was. I wanted. Security. With you.' (p. 24)) the more she dismisses them by explaining how she understands their underlying meaning: 'You Essentially said you wanted to reduce your income tax. [. . .] And inherit my pension. [. . .] That you can decide what to do with my body if I happen to die in a different country' (pp. 24–25). At the end they arrive at an impasse as they both realize that they want different things out of their relationship.

The third scene, 'Revolutionize the Work. (Engage with It.)', shifts the focus from the private sphere of love to the public domain of work. The linguistic battle staged here concerns an employee and her manager: the former has just let the latter know that she wants to take Mondays off work to be able to spend time in the countryside and sleep more. Her defiance expresses a resistance to be productive thus challenging the capitalist structures that govern work relations. Her manager sees work as a one-way street where you need to serve the system in order to succeed. Because of this capitalist understanding of success, the manager fails to empathize with the employee's need to work less where she should be trying to prove herself in order to secure promotion. In trying to understand her, the manager rehearses several sexist clichés, such as, 'Are you pregnant?', 'Are you having a Mental Fucking Breakdown?', 'Do you want to be paid as much as [. . .] the boys?' (p. 32), but also tries to appease her by attempting to construct the illusion that she can find moments of leisure at work, such as through spa days or using the office's vending machines, or through bribes such as the offer of a 'work handbag' (p. 31). The female character resists such offers in order to reclaim her body and labour from being owned and exploited by capitalism; she wins the argument with the final line: 'I'll see you on Tuesday' (p. 34).

The final scene, 'Revolutionise the Body (Make it Sexually Available. Constantly).', blurs the line between private and public spheres by placing the female body at the centre of public scrutiny. There are at least three voices in the scene, one of which is a female who is being interrogated for interrupting the consumerist flow of a supermarket by staging a protest: the woman is accused of lying on the floor revealing her naked body next to a crushed watermelon with her hand on her knickers and 'surrounded by cereal boxes and potatoes' (p. 39). The supermarket employees use customer-service language mixed with abusive body-shaming (descriptions of 'curdled flab', 'bingo wings', 'muffin top', 'pork belly', and 'chicken thighs' (p. 40)). The play compares the capitalist freedom to buy products from all over the world to women's sexual freedom. By highlighting the ongoing sexualization of women's bodies and their subjection to vocabularies of disgust and shaming if they fail to meet particular standards of beauty, the scene questions the possibility of liberating women's bodies from the continuous cycles of violence and abuse. The scene closes with a dark and powerful monologue that suggests the impossibility for women to escape capitalist and male exploitation: after failing to fortify her body against male invasion, the female performer now tries to obliterate the borders between her body and other bodies and make herself hyper visible so that: 'there Is no in to come into, you cannot overpower it because I have given it you cannot rape it because I choose it you cannot take because I give it and because I choose it I choose it I choose it' (p. 42).

Act 2

In contrast to Act 1, Act 2 is written as a continuous scene divided into seven short sections. The structural principle of a revolution manual is maintained with titles indicating different sets of instructions such as 'Revolutionize the World (Don't Reproduce)', 'Revolutionize the Work (Don't Do it)', 'Revolutionize the Body / The Language (Stop Speaking)' but the stage directions indicate that 'the titles do not break the action' (p. 43). The act unfolds as a confrontation between two women, Grandma and her daughter Dinah who was abandoned by her mother at the age of four and has not met her since. The third woman in the scene is Dinah's daughter, Agnes, who assumes the role of a passive observer and who 'has started to stop talking, she won't eat, she won't lift her hands, she can't keep hold of a thing, not a thing, she is starting to disappear entirely' (p. 44). The purpose of Dinah's and Agnes's visit to Grandma is that Dinah wants her mother to reassure Agnes that 'she came from somewhere good', which will help to improve Agnes's health (p. 44). Despite Dinah's search for the kindness and affection she was deprived of as a child, Grandma insists that she had no children (p. 46).

Here, the play seems to return to some of the key tenets of second-wave feminism that are still relevant in the twenty-first century and to question to what extent they improved the lives of the next generation of women. As can be observed throughout the different sections, the play deals with the themes of language, work, reproduction and the body, which are exposed as salient issues that also plague younger women as much as Grandma's generation. The idea of sisterhood that operated as a vehicle of solidarity and community among women during the period of second-wave feminism here seems to be replaced by an absence of love and intense feelings of fatigue, exhaustion and disgust. Grandma's insistence to separate herself from any familial ties indicates an individualistic approach to identity and a lack of affection. Agnes is so tired that she drops the bluebells and then vomits in a later scene bringing disgust to the character/actor playing Grandma. She speaks only in one scene entitled 'Revolutionize the Language (That Word Does not Exist Here)', but only in unconventional language, which reveals the lack of a compass that would offer meaning to her life. Dinah tries to be more empathetic towards her mother and to understand the reasons why she left her. In doing so, she imagines different scenarios that would justify Grandma's actions, which rehearse some traditional gender clichés associated with sexual abuse, physical or mental illness: 'You got trapped. [. . .] Daddy beat you up', 'You'd fallen very terribly gravely ill', 'You were depressed. Contemplating suicide' (pp. 48–9). As Grandma denies all these versions, Dinah continues her interrogation with questions that reflect further anxieties about childbirth and motherhood, such as the impact on the climate and the female body, or the failure to perform a caring and loving mothering role that has been ascribed to women as 'natural'. Rather than providing us with answers to Dinah's questions, the scene ends with Grandma and Agnes chopping their tongues with their knife and fork; this striking tableau reminds us of the cost of endorsing individualism and how it impacts different generations of women, as well as the failure to articulate the real experiences of women within a traditional form such as a realist family scene.

Act 3

Act 3 appears as a single scene under the title 'Galvanize', which addresses a further call to arms for women to take action against oppressive forces whilst also implying the need to disturb and shock in order to remove us from complacency. Shifting focus from the family unit to the wider community of women, Act 3 is still preoccupied with enduring feminist debates regarding rape, the objectification and consumption of the female body in the media and everyday life, children's anorexia and pornography. Here the play seems to take on an altogether different form to contain the scene's incendiary quality. On the page, the script is written in the style of fragmented speech split into different columns to indicate overlapping dialogue and simultaneous actions or vignettes on stage. The space is even more fluid than in the previous acts and the pace is noticeably faster; these features encourage a multitude of voices as well as chaos and messiness on stage as the actors are asked to 'be in more than one scene' and acknowledge the difficulty of doing so (p. 52). The form of this scene gives the impression of a social media feed replete with incomplete and contradictory debates generated by a cacophony of voices.

Although the different vignettes might seem to be disjointed at first read, this act is mainly preoccupied with debunking the myth that women have achieved freedom of choice and agency over their bodies. This is particularly evident during the dialogue between a woman whose house (that stands as a metaphor for her body) has been violated and a police officer who insists on telling her that she cannot prove it. This vignette speaks to the huge difficulties for women to prove that they have been sexually abused without being accused of being responsible for it:

- [. . .] that could of course just be a Choice you've made in terms of your living arrangements [. . .]
- Um, the uh, my windows are all smashed
- Yeah, but again, who's to say

  You didn't do that yourself
- I've got blood all over my legs
- [. . .]
- Yeah, but it's just that there's no evidence [. . .]

p. 58

In another vignette a woman mechanically repeats the line 'my choice' fifty-five times whilst running around (p. 62), to then conclude 'it really Is Better and safest and Nicest for everyone if You stay Indoors because otherwise you might get attacked and we can all go Outdoors but because none of You will be Outdoors then none of Us will be able to attack you so that's Nicest' (pp. 62–63). This speech unravels whilst a wedding ceremony takes place between a twelve-year-old girl and her rapist (p. 62). These two juxtaposing images capture yet again the tensions between the private and the public sphere; they remind us both how women's oppression has remained largely invisible throughout history as well as the feminist backlash created when such issues are aired in public and disturb patriarchal structures.

The scene returns to the feelings of exhaustion of Act 2, reminding us of women's continuous emotional labour and struggles to defend their right to own their body; this exhaustion interlaces with anger as a galvanizing force that can destroy patriarchal structures: as one of the actors/characters declares, 'it's a Massive Fuck Off Explosion we're after. Because really. Really there's nowhere else to go' (p. 60). This anger also takes the form of a critique of postfeminism that has allowed women to become complacent and individualistic and to neglect nurturing the fruits of their previous feminist labour. Characters expose the artificiality of the principles of choice and progress and express regret for how choice became a motto that promotes individualism: an actor/character teaches another actor/character how to repeat the line 'my choice' whereas, at the end of the scene, a female character exclaims: 'your choice your choice your choice and my choice have turned out to be not the fertile soil we thought we were standing two feet apart upon but dry and arid and empty and alone [. . .]' (p. 66). As already foreshadowed, the scene ends with an explosion that interrupts the final climactic speech and is described in the stage directions as, '*Loud noise. It is cold. It is bright. And then it is black.*' (p. 66). This suspenseful moment gives the impression that the revolution is underway and offers some hope for change.

Act 4

Revolt ends with a one-and-a-half page act, which begins with a fierce desire for global change. As per the note to the scene, it requires four women who share their ideas and enthusiasm about the radical possibilities of their revolt: 'We're going to dismantle the monetary system, [. . .] And overthrow the government [. . .] We'll expect other countries to follow suit. [. . .] And we take over the airwaves, the televisions, the Internet, etcetera. And we'll eradicate all men' (pp. 67–8). In as much as it envisages a transition to an equal world, the scene also shows how revolutions are bound to fail; the characters question the success of their revolt, expressing feelings of fear and uncertainty. One of them points out that the other character sounds sad:

- It won't work if you're sad
- It won't work if you aren't.
- It failed. The whole world failed at it. It could have been so brilliant. How strange of you not to feel sad.
- Who knew that life could be so awful.

p. 68

The feelings of sadness and disillusionment at the end of the play capture yet again the play's critique of the past failings of feminism and fear for patriarchy's resilience, inviting the audience to contemplate the idea of revolt as an inevitability and a utopian vision.

Staging *Revolt. She said. Revolt again.* and the play's performance history

Although often demanding, the play's stylistic devices offer immense creative freedom to directors and actors in terms of characterization and stage design as characters, time and space remain unspecified throughout. As per the author's note at the beginning of the play, set and props should be minimal and the offstage space where costume and make-up changes are taking place 'should be as visible to the audience as possible' (p. 7). The piece also allows room for a playful exploration of performer-audience relationship – for example, through direct audience address. The actors switch between characters without particular investment in psychological characterization; age or gender do not matter, which undermines any sense of realism, even in scenes that might approximate a realist aesthetic. Most notably in Act 2, it is suggested that Grandma could be played by a young woman as it 'doesn't matter if GRANDMA looks very young' (p. 43). Although gender seems to be fluid, the play makes clear that gender parity on stage is maintained, challenging the histories of women's representation as sexual objects and the dominance of male bodies on stage. The stage directions indicate that there should be at least one female character in each scene and that 'If a woman has to get a bit naked at any point, then the men should get naked also to redress the balance' (p. 7).

The play often instructs the actors to step out of their character, creating uncertainty whether it is the actor or the character that speaks; they often repeat the line 'I don't understand' to punctuate their personal confusion and hesitation towards their circumstances. These devices flesh out the wider theme of uncertainty that the play explores in relation to revolt: the uncertainty of revolt's success, but also how revolting against patriarchal and capitalist structures might lead to a global destabilization. The feelings of exhaustion and tiredness that are repeated throughout the play are further complemented by the actors' real fatigue on stage as they have to perform physical tasks (such as running around) that put strain on their body. The play also draws attention to the materiality and the liveness of the performance, which can be further enhanced by additional directorial choices. These were highlighted in the play's

New York premiere at Soho Rep theatre directed by Lileana Blain-Cruz. Upon entry, the audience had a brief backstage view witnessing the actors getting ready for the show by performing routine exercises, such as stretching and drinking water. They were also confronted with strong visual and olfactory stimuli, such as when an actress scooped pieces of watermelon over her body to then offer the audience 'clean slices on fine china' (Phillips, 2016, p. 671).

In as much as character and setting remain fluid and malleable, the delivery of the text needs to be approached with great precision. The script provides very specific instructions in terms of punctuation and overlapping speech, which in turn demand careful and detailed work on each scene's different rhythms: dashes stand for change of speaker and forward slash (/) for overlapping speech. Full stops also indicate a pause, which can last from a 'single beat or ten minutes' (p. 7), whereas the absence of a full stop 'denotes a kind of interruption' (p. 7). As the play does not invest in characterization, but rather in the theme of power through language, actors and directors are invited to clearly define different character dynamics by paying attention to the speech actions underpinning each line.

In addition to the play's freedom with character, creative teams can also experiment with setting and stagecraft. Frequent references to ordinary objects, such as watermelon, bluebells and potatoes, acquire significance and constantly appear on stage as metaphors for women's experience whilst place often remains unspecified and fluid. For the play's world premiere at the Royal Shakespeare Company's Midsummer Mischief festival in 2014, which was revived at the Edinburgh Fringe Festival in 2016, director Erica Whyman divided the stage into separate character spaces, emphasizing the characters' isolation. Evoking the theme of revolution, she capitalized on colour and objects using red fire buckets containing red dust and paint, a fire extinguisher, red sand, red paint and a watermelon on stage. As the piece progressed, the space became messier, with the actors splattering paint against the black wall, chopping the watermelon with an axe and sifting sand on the floor.

Costume can also play a key role in serving the play's plasticity with character and location. For the play's Luxembourg premiere in 2016, director Sophie Langevin and visual artist and designer Sophie Van den Keybus gave the actors stylized costumes, such as long white shirts, thick socks and leggings, sleeveless plastic dresses and aprons, which they used as accessories that constantly changed the signification of character and place.

The play's fluidity, precision with language and rhythm lends itself to explore musicality; several productions have experimented with different possibilities of live music as soundscape. For example, for its French (Villeneuve, 2016) and German (Berliner Ensemble, 2018) premieres, directors Arnaud Ankaert and Christina Tscharyiski respectively included live music on stage, the former giving a 'rock concert' edge and the latter putting well-known female rapper Ebow on stage. In the play's Denmark premiere (Husets Theater, 2018), the stage comprised an ensemble of five actors, a piano and several microphone stands placed close to each other, creating a live soundscape from the spoken text.

Critical reception

Revolt received much praise from theatre critics, playwrights and scholars. The *Daily Telegraph*'s critic Dominic Cavendish (2014) described the play as 'a cluster-bomb of subversion' while the *New York Times* critic Ben Brantley (2016) compared it to John Osborne's *Look Back in Anger* (1956) for its 'anarchic fury', as well as to 'the form-bending virtuosity of Caryl Churchill'. For the *Guardian*'s Michael Billington (2014), the play demonstrated that 'Birch has a gift for radical experiment in the style of Caryl Churchill and Sarah Kane'. In a similar vein, Aleks Sierz (2016) aligns Birch's unconventional style with Kane, Churchill and Martin Crimp, praising the play for its 'enormous technical skill and sense of emotional truth'. On the other hand, Steward Pringle (2016) from *The Stage* criticized the play for addressing only 'upwardly middle class women'.

Reviewers across different geographical contexts also seemed to agree on the play's exceptional craft, as well as expressing their admiration for its contemporary relevance with #MeToo. Similarly, academic essays on the play have particularly focused on its uses of anger as a potent feminist tool that creates 'mischief' in order to dismantle patriarchy, postfeminism and capitalism, and its revolutionary language (Fragkou, 2020; 2021; Escoda). For Dan Rebellato (2017) in particular, *Revolt* belongs to a wider post-apocalyptic sentiment in British playwriting that challenges realism, inviting us to imagine the end of capitalism.

Revolt's positive critical reception and revivals in the UK, as well as its numerous international productions and translations have put the play on the map of the international playwriting scene; this recognition highlights its relevance across different Western contexts and bears the promise of *Revolt* becoming a modern theatre classic which will be widely studied and staged in the years to come.

List of key productions

UK: Royal Shakespeare Company, The Other Place, Courtyard Theatre, Stratford-upon-Avon, June 2014. Transferred to the Theatre Upstairs, Royal Court, London, July 2014. Directed by Erica Whyman.

Revival: Traverse Theatre, Edinburgh Fringe, August 2016. Directed by Erica Whyman.

France: La Manufacture-Patinoire, Avignon, July 2016. Directed by Arnaud Anckaert.

U.S.: Soho Rep, New York. April 2016. Directed by Lileana Blain-Cruz.

Australia: Malthouse Theatre, Melbourne, June 2017. Directed by Janice Muller.

Luxembourg: Théâtre du Centaure, Luxembourg, January 2018. Directed by Sophie Langevin.

Denmark: Husets Theater, Copenhagen, February 2018. Directed by Marina Bouras and Jens Albinus.

Germany: Berliner Ensemble, Berlin, October 2018. Directed by Christina Tscharyiski.

Works cited

Aston, E. (1995) *An Introduction to Feminism and Theatre*, London and New York: Routledge.

Aston, E. (2021) *Restaging Feminisms*, Cham: Palgrave.

Bailes, S. J. (2011) *Performance, Theatre and the Poetics of Failure*, London: Routledge.

Benedict, D. (1997) 'The Mother of Reinvention', *Independent*, 19 April, Arts Section.

Billington, M. (2014) 'Midsummer Mischief review – RSC's radical billing is witty and inventive', *Guardian*, 23 June. Available online: https://www.theguardian.com/stage/2014/jun/23/midsummer-mischief-royal-shakespeare-company-stratford-review (accessed 1 August 2022).

Brantley, B. (2016) 'Review: Revolt. She said. Revolt again. Captures the fury of modern womanhood', *New York Times*, 19 April 2016. Available online: https://www.nytimes.com/2016/04/20/theater/review-revolt-she-said-revolt-again-captures-the-fury-of-modern-womanhood.html (accessed 1 August 2022).

Case, S. E. (2008) *Feminism and Theatre*. Rev. edn, Basingstoke: Palgrave.

Cavendish, D. (2014) 'Midsummer Mischief, The Other Place at the Courtyard Theatre, Stratford-upon-Avon, review', *Telegraph*, 22 June. Available online: https://www.telegraph.co.uk/culture/theatre/theatre-reviews/10917888/Midsummer-Mischief-The-Other-Place-at-the-Courtyard-Theatre-Stratford-upon-Avon-review.html (accessed 1 August 2022)

Escoda Agustí, C. (forthcoming) 'Revolt. She said. Revolt again (2014)', in V. Angelaki and D. Rebellato (eds), *The Cambridge Companion to British Playwriting since 1945*, Cambridge: Cambridge University Press.

Fragkou, M. (2020) 'debbie tucker green and Alice Birch: "Angry Feminists" on the European Stage', in M. Delgado, B. Lease and D. Rebellato (eds), *Contemporary European Playwrights*, 334–51, London: Routledge.

Fragkou, M. (2021) '"Feeling Feminism": Politics of Mischief in Contemporary Women's Theatre', in M. Aragay, C. Delgado Garcia, C. and M. Middeke (eds), *Affects in Twenty-First Century British Theatre: Exploring Feeling on Page and Stage*, 127–47, London: Springer.

Gorman, S. (2021) *Women in Performance: Repurposing Failure*, London and New York: Routledge.

Philipps, E. (2016) 'Review of Revolt. She said. Revolt again', *Theatre Journal*, 68 (4): 670–2.

Pringle, S. (2016) 'Revolt. She said. Revolt again', *The Stage*, 20 August 2016, Available online: https://www.thestage.co.uk/reviews/2016/revolt-she-said-revolt-again-review-at-traverse-theatre-edinburgh-falls-short/ (accessed 1 August 2022).

Rebellato, D. (2017) 'Of an apocalyptic tone recently adopted in theatre: British drama, violence and writing', *Sillages Critiques* [En ligne], 22, http://journals.openedition.org/sillagescritiques/4798 (accessed 1 August 2022).

Sierz, A. (2016) 'Revolt. She said. Revolt again. Shoreditch Town Hall', *Aleks Sierz*, 2 September. Available online: https://www.sierz.co.uk/reviews/revolt-she-said-revolt-again-shoreditch-town-hall/ (accessed 1 August 2022).

Revolt. She said. Revolt again.

For my Mum.

It wouldn't have come out the way it has without many
women, but namely:

Susan Brownmiller

Helen Goalen and Abbi Greenland

Nina Power

Valerie Solanas

Erica Whyman

I want to thank the RSC – Mark, Claire, Réjane, Collette,
Pippa and Sarah

Giles
and Sam.

Revolt. She said. Revolt again. was first produced by the Royal Shakespeare Company as part of the *Midsummer Mischief* Festival in 2014. This production was revived at The Other Place on 2 August 2016 as part of the *Making Mischief* Festival before transferring to the Traverse, Edinburgh and Shoreditch Town Hall. The cast was as follows:

Revolt. She said. Revolt again.

Company	**Robert Boulter**
	Emmanuella Cole
	Emma Fielding
	Beth Park
Director	**Erica Whyman**
Designer	**Madeleine Girling**
Lighting Designer	**Claire Gerrens**
Sound Designer	**Jonathan Ruddick**
Voice and Text Work	**Anna McSweeney**
Assistant Director	**Hannah Joss**
Casting Director	**Matthew Dewsbury**
Production Manager	**Julian Cree**
Costume Supervisor	**Zarah Meherali**
Company Stage Manager	**Jenny Grand**
First Technician Sound	**Jake Smith**
First Technician Light	**Jamie Spirito**
Producer	**Claire Birch**

This text may differ slightly from the play as performed.

Consider the idea that offstage should be as visible to the audience as possible. 'The actors' are another set of characters. Shoes – particularly high ones – should be taken off and on, lipstick removed and reapplied. If any vomiting, crying or shouting needs to happen offstage, the audience should be able to glimpse it at the very least.

There shouldn't be any set. The play should be performable without any props.

There should be at least one female character (that should probably be played by a female actor) in every scene.

If a woman has to get a bit naked at any point, then the men should get naked also to redress the balance.

A dash – indicates a change of speaker.

/ Denotes the overlapping of speech.

Words in square brackets [ ] are not spoken.

The absence of a full stop at the end of a line denotes a kind of interruption – the lines should run at speed.

The use of a full stop on a line on its own suggests a pause – whether this is a single beat or ten minutes depends on what feels right.

The spacing of the dialogue, the use of upper and lower case letters and the punctuation is all there to help the actor in terms of the pacing and the weight of their words.

If the titles are shown, in Act Two they should stack up on top of one another in some way.

Most importantly, this play should not be well behaved.

Act One

Revolutionize the Language. (Invert It.)

–   I don't understand.

      .

      I don't understand how you do what you do to me.

–   I don't Do anything to you.

      I Don't.

      I do

      Whatever I do

      And whatever You think or feel or

      Whatever

      Is all you – is All you.

–   I want to make love to you.

      You are a Brilliant Bright Bright thing – do you have any idea
      what your shoulders, bare like that, do to me, do to my
      structure, to my insides – I want to make a brooch out of your
      hair and your pupils and your ribs – and I know that sounds
      fucking – but I want to pin that to my heart and let my blood
      drain I'm done it's You let's Everybody Out Now World I Am
      Gone.

      .

      I bought you bluebells.

      I made him wrap them – I had the little man wrap them in
      brown paper for you – I want – and I have been thinking – All
      Day Long

That I want to make love to you – don't move, don't move, just for a second just
could you stay exactly where you are?

– I

– You look completely perfect

– Can I

– You look completely and utterly perfect – stay exactly as you are

.

– Can I just

put this down?

– No

– Are you – ?

– It's your body – it's the line of your body

– Yeah, but can I

– It's the line your neck makes

– Makes?

– Your hip, there like that

– It's just my / hip

– / Is perfection

– I'm just.

I'm going to move now

Because there's all this [mess] to clear up and.

– You're perfection.

– What's that [noise] – is that a

– Perfection

–   Nightingale or a

–   Complete Perfection

–   Wine? Do you want wine?

–   All through dinner, all I could think about was getting you
    home and making love to you – the only thought in my head,
    the whole way through that fucking cheese course was That
    mole
    on your jaw
    and how I wanted to lick it.

–   You ate loads of cheese

–   I was thinking about licking your mole

–   You ate an Enormous amount of cheese – I was beginning to
    feel Worried, I was considering Expressing Concern – you
    physically Put me off cheese, I could barely finish my
    watermelon – d'you want a drink or

–   I can barely hear what you're saying – I'm obsessed – I barely
    heard a word Anyone said – all I could think about was
    fucking you

–   They were talking about North Korea

–   Your lips. That lip.

–   Over cheese. I thought you were really into it, I thought you
    were really Absorbed –
    you looked – they were talking about prison camps and
    Genocide – about Mass
    Genocide – you looked. You Looked Moved.

–   All I could think about was coming home, laying you down
    upon that bed

–   That bit about that family who'd had all their fingers cut off,
    I thought

–   Thinking about you and

–   I thought you were were Welling Up

–   Laying you down upon that bed
      And making love to you.

–   .

–   And making love to you

–   .

–   Laying you down. And making love to you.

–   Or

–   No or

–   Or

–   There Is no Or – there is no other option

–   Yes but

–   I want to make Love to you

–   Or
      With?

–   .

With.

With.

.

With you – make love – I want to make love With you

–   Yeah?

–   Yeah

–   Yeah

–   Yes

–   Aaaaand?

–   And, yes, and and kissing you, I want to kiss you – With you,
    I want to kiss With / you

–   / Kissing you is fine

–   Kissing you and and holding you and putting my hand at the
    bottom of your back
    and and
    What?

–   It's the Putting, the Putting sounds

–   Putting

–   Something about it sounds

–   Putting? putting? putting. putting. putt ting. put ting I

–   No no no no, okay, no you're right, you're right, putting is
    fine, putting is Good, putting is – you're putting – putting –
    putting your hand at the bottom of my back

–   And and I'm kissing you

–   Yeah

–   I'm kissing you and and pressing you to me – can I say
    pressing?

–   If I feel like I want to be pressed – which, now I think of it,
    yes, I do – then yes

–   Good

–   Really good

–   Pressing you to me so Fucking Hard – is that

–   Keep going

–   That when you fall back into your own space the marks of me
    are all over you

–   And me on you

–   Like a a a a an imprint and a

- And me on you

- And I'm kissing your neck

- Marks of me are on you though

- I'm kissing, I'm kissing hard and I'm running my hands up and down your sides again and again and again and

- And I'm on you

- You're on me

- I'm on you

- And I want to feel you Shiver – shiver in a good way in a brilliant way

- Okay

- Yeah and and then, then I'm going to peel your dress off – slow – and and don't laugh

- Not laugh / ing

- / And you

- Not laughing but I'm also not a potato

- You can peel my clothes off

- You are also not a potato this is not potato / sex

- / And I'm I'm kissing you, all over

- Mmmm?

- Yeah I'm kissing you all over and and I'm going to spread your legs

- Oh?

- Or you will spread them. When you are ready to spread them.

- Mmmm

- Uh huh

—   What was that

—   I don't know – so so

—   Or you could spread yours

—   Or. Yes. Or. I. Yes. I suppose I could spread mine.

—   Yes, why don't you spread yours?

—   Okay. Yes. Okay. I will spread my legs

—   Yeah?

—   Yeah

—   Yeah.

    Spread them.

—   But first. First. Could you spread yours?

—   No.

—   Alright. Alright.

—   Spread them.

—   I. Um. I don't want to Spread them – could / we not say
    Spread

—   / You don't want / to spread them now

—   / sort of sounds like margarine or

—   Open?

—   Open.

    Yes. YES.

    Open. Open is good

—   Open

—   So, so you open, we both open, but I open Your legs

—   You open my / legs

—   / Your legs and I want to Lick you, I want to extend my tongue
      and I want to lick you

—   I'll lick you back

—   .

      Okay.

—   Yeah, I'll extend my tongue

—   And my tongue is up inside you

—   And I'll put my tongue up inside you

—   And my fingers are up inside you now

—   And I'll put my fingers up inside you

—   And and – where? Where are / your fingers

—   / Up inside your mouth, your arse, your

—   Don't say arse

—   Bum

—   Don't say bum, I can't do

—   Your Back Alley

—   I have my hand up inside you

She spits.

—   Then I have my whole fist up inside you

—   Ummmm

—   You Like that

—   I feel Conflicted about

—   Then take your hand out

—   I'm going to fuck you

—   I'm going to fuck you straight back

—   And I'm going to take my cock / and

–   / AndI'mgoingtotakemyvaginaandputitOnyouFIRST

–   What was that?

–   I get there first.

–   Yeah?

–   Yeah I am On you before you are In me

–   Are you

–   I'm going to take my vagina

–   Hang on

–   I'm taking my vagina

–   You can't Take your vagina

–   I am Taking My Vagina

–   You cannot Take a a a a a Gap

–   My Vagina is an Organ, my Vagina is not a Gap

–   It

–   How fucking Dare you – you are lucky to be anywhere
     Near my / Organ

–   / Your Organ is On My Organ

–   My Organ is On Your Organ

–   It's on my Big Hard Organ

–   It's All over it

–   Yeah, I'm pushing

–   I'm pushing back

–   And I'm pushing

–   And I'm Slamming it back down with my organ

–   And I'm

–   And I'm Enveloping you

- Like. As in
- I'm Surrounding you
- Surround me, okay, yes, yes Surround me
- I am Consuming you
- Baby consume me
- And I – don't call me baby – I am Gorging on you, I am Making You My Dildo
- And so the the so / the
- / I am Drowning and Suffocating and Overwhelming you with my Giant Organ
- Well, it's cos / it's
- / I am Scissoring you
- That's
- I am Fucking Scissoring you to bits
- Is that
- I am Scissoring and Slicing you
- Then I am Screwing you
- And I am Spannering you
- I
- I am Completely Spannering you and I am Jumping you and Hiding you and

   Chomping down upon you
- Not what I
- I am Blanketing and Locking you and Draining The
  Life of you with my Massive
  Structured
  Beautifully built
  Almighty Vagina.

.

Alright?

Are you Alright?

– .

– No?

– I just I

– No?

Then I will Take Your Penis

Sorry.

sorry.

– I. I. with the um. I. I feel. I.

– sorry I will take my Vagina. Off your penis.

Okay?

Revolutionize the World. (Do Not Marry.)

– I don't understand why you're so – I just. I.

I wasn't expecting it.

.

It's not the. Sweetheart. It's not the uhhh. Sort of thing.

You Expect. Or look Out for.

Or.

Or.

Think About.

Ever.

We've never talked about it.

Ever.

Except at my Mum's uhhhh funeral Actually, and because it wasn't

Because that wasn't a

Romantic – I didn't – a Romantic Setting, I'd sort of maybe not really registered that as a a a a a Thing you might be – I mean, I was trying to talk about Anything so that I didn't have to think about her Dead Fucking Body the other side of a a a curtain from us and our conversation and those those Brown Shoes you were wearing, those totally awful Brown shoes you'd Found and put on and worn to my Mother's funeral as though your sole objective that day was to make me Cry More Not Less I'm sorry, I don't mean that – you're my world my yadda yadda but the point is so I, I mean, we could have been talking about about Anything or or or or Any – so, so if that was you being Serious, if that was
you introducing that concept To our relationship at that point then I did not take that seriously and I'm sorry.

.

Except I'm Not fucking sorry because that was astonishingly poorly timed on your part.

.

I'm sorry. I am sorry for my language – I'm sorry about [that]

.

It was.

It was – I'm trying to find a

Words to.

.

What just happened was like

Was like.

It was like – what it was like was, was

Okay. So.

What I'm Feeling is.

What it was Like was if – Imagine if, okay – Imagine

If I just like, One Day

This is just – and this is just me Expressing how I'm feeling

Imagine if I one day – and this is it – if I one day

Waltzed in and was like. Like. Poppet. Sweetheart.
Nightingale of mine and heart's desire. I love you. I love you
to the edges of this earth and back, I love you body and heart
and soul, I love you and I reckon to express this love, we
should go and blow up the local Sainsbury's.

.

And then I Presented you
with a Massive Bomb
Upon a Vest.

.

On Bended Knee.

.

And Prior to this, okay, Prior to this moment, this Bended
Knee moment, let's imagine that the only conversation we had
ever had about Bombing or or or Suicide Bombers in any
sense, was, in fact, a sort of vague chat in which maybe one of
us might have expressed slightly hesitant but not entirely
unpredictable – given our bleeding-heart liberalism – empathy
towards said suicide bombers who had lost everything in a war
that you and I from our privileged position understand very
little about in any real sense at least – and I'm proud of that
empathy, that empathy is a Good Thing – but Imagine though,

imagine, that that slightly vague experience had been, in fact, the only conversation we had Ever had about bombing and then in I stroll with a suicide vest and suggest that we go and blow up the local supermarket in the sort of tone that suggested that that had been the plan all along – I mean, imagine your surprise.

Imagine

your surprise.

.

–   I didn't Suggest that we blow up a supermarket / together

–   / Of course you didn't – that was a fu – that was a Metaphor, that was a

     I wish you had.

.

–   We've been to weddings together

–   We have watched suicide bomb reports on the news together but that doesn't

–   I just told you I loved you

–   No you didn't

–   I just told you I loved you

–   Nope

–   And that I wanted to spend the rest of my life with you

–   Presenting me with an enormous diamond. Or bomb. Does not mean those things.

–   You Love diamonds.

–   I feel Concerned

     About where diamonds come from.

.

—   I just want you to be my wife, it's not a.

     It wasn't a.

     I didn't Find those shoes – I Bought those shoes specifically for –

     .

     We can get a Different ring.

     I want to have a life with you – I just said I want to have a life with you

—   No you didn't

—   All I said was I wanted to live my life Next to yours

—   No you didn't

—   That I wanted to love you forever

—   That isn't what you said

—   I just said that I just wanted to commit to you

—   Nnnno

—   I said that you're The most important human being to me

—   No

—   That you're a really important person in my life

—   Not what you said

—   That you're a person in my life

—   Nope

—   That you make me smile every time I see you

—   No

—   That you you make me laugh more than anyone

—   No

—   That I want to to buy Dogs and then bury those dogs in a back garden we share

– No

– I said I wanted to do my online food shop with you and go on all my main holidays with you and and

– Did not hear you say a single one of those words

– That I want to bring up small humans that we sort of might make together

– No

– That I want to share values and dinners and and baths with you

– No

– That I want I want
  What I said was. I wanted. Security. With you.

– Those words didn't come out of your mouth

       .

– I just said

– No

– All I Said was

– Nah

– It.

– No you didn't

– I'm. I want. It's. I.

       .

– You Essentially said you wanted to reduce your income tax.

–   .

  What?

– And inherit my pension.

– I did not

– That you can decide what to do with my body if I

 happen to die in another country

– Those words did not – another what / now

– That you want me to give up my name

– You can you can / Keep your

– / That you want to turn me into Chattel

– If – I just

– A thing to be traded

– Can we

– That I am to become your possession, your property, a thing
 you own – given to you by a man I don't really speak to
 anymore holding a bunch of fucking bluebells and wearing a
 meringue in some kind of enormous shaming event in which
 I am supposed to be a Silent Walking Symbol of virginity yet
 simultaneously be Totally Relaxed about all the sex we are
 having whilst you get to walk around Doing All The Talking
 in a suit

– It doesn't Mean those things anymore

– What does it mean then?

  .

– I want to marry you.

 I want you to be my wife.

 My partner.

  .

– I am not entirely sure I believe in those things.

– Is this.

 Are you.

 I want to marry

I want to

I want

I.

Is. Is this. is this just occurring to you Now?

—   No.

Yes.

Maybe.

I don't know.

Revolutionize the Work. (Engage with It.)

—   I um. I don't. Sorry. No. I don't understand.

—   That's fine

—   No, it's not fine.

—   I feel very fine about it.

—   Yes, You feel – You feel fine. I do not feel fine about it.

    .

—   I don't want to work Mondays.

That feels fairly straightforward.

—   Okay. And can you tell me Why you don't want to work Mondays?

—   I want to get more sleep

—   On Mondays?

—   I want to sleep more

—   We all want to sleep more

—   Then maybe we should all do something about that.

I want to walk my dogs more. I have inherited a house in the
countryside that has a path that goes from my doorstep and
leads through the garden that is just potatoes and then
bluebells – when it is the right time for bluebells – and that
path then leads to fields and keeps going through fields and
past a brook and those fields, they back onto a little wood
where there are larks and nightingales and I want to walk in
that wood. With my dogs. On a Monday.

It's very beautiful.

–   I know it is. I know it is, you've had me and my girlfriend
over for dinner, it's very fucking beautiful, it felt very fucking
beautiful as we stood in your potato patch, I don't – .

    .

I'm sorry.

    .

–   I don't want to do that anymore. I don't want to cook for
hours. I don't want to have people over for dinner anymore
because I want to Sleep more and I want to walk my dogs
more often in the woods.

    .

–   We've put vending machines in the corridors.

–   I don't care.

–   We've put vending machines in and we're building a gym in
the basement.

–   I don't want those things.

–   You're being very obtuse.

–   I'm being very clear.

    .

–   Are you pregnant?

−   Do I Look pregnant?

−   .

    I'd believe you if you said you were. You don't look
    Not pregnant.

−   I'm not pregnant.

−   Are you Trying to get pregnant?

−   That's not really any of your business

−   It Is if I need to recruit someone else

−   I'm not trying to get pregnant

    .

−   Do you Want to Try to get pregnant

−   What I want to try to do is not your − no. No, I don't want to
    do that

−   Women want that − it's okay

−   I don't want that

−   You're a real career girl?

−   I just want more sleep

−   Do you want to do a course? Is that it? Do you want to further
    your studies?

−   Not really.

−   Ah. Okay. Okay. You're not where you thought you
    Might be

−   No, I'm not, but that's not the

−   Where you thought you Could be

−   That's not

−   In fact, because − and this is, this is really − I'm the First
    person in my family to go to university, okay. And now look.

A course might help you tap into whatever it is you

– I'm the first person in my family to keep all their fingers past the age of twenty-one.

.

– We really appreciate your labour.

– I'm fine.

– You don't Seem fine

– I'm really fine

– It's okay that you're Not fine

– I am fine.

– It's okay. We're talking about some intense things. We can use one of the Relax rooms

– I'm fine.

– You really care about this

– I don't care. I'm just being clear with you.

– You Sound a little bit like you care.

– I

– And we can help with that. Perhaps you should look at doing a course.

– I just want more time off

– Mondays off

– Mondays off. Initially.

.

– Are you Ill?

– No

– Okay, is it cancer?

– No

– Is it terminal? Is it piles, do you have haemorrhoids?

– Not at the minute

– That's disgusting

– I just want to work less. Don't you?

– Are you having a Mental Fucking Breakdown?

.

I'm sorry. I apologise for my language.

The vending machines have chocolate and fizzy drinks and sandwiches and flavoured water in them.

– I don't care about those things.

– What if you could bring your dogs into the work environment? Would that make things better? Would you feel better about working Mondays then?

– I want to walk my dogs through things that grow in the woods.

– There are trees near here. You could walk your dogs, your – what kind of dogs

– Pitbulls.

.

– Are you

– Deadly.

.

– You could walk your Pitbulls by the trees near here in your lunchbreak and get a sandwich from the vending machine and you could watch them Piss all over the grass and then you could go to the gym after your shift and read one of the complimentary magazines after your cool down

- I don't think you're listening.

- We've put a bar on the rooftop terrace and we're doing Happy Hour Fridays. We could do Happy Hour Mondays as well, would that help? There are beers and wines and the spritzers and the Cosmopolitans are very popular with the girls, we can bring Happy Hour in on a Monday as well, if you like, and we could relax the No Dogs and the No Smoking rules because we want it to be fun, we want it to be a genuinely fun working environment

- It's work. It's not a real bar.

- It's the work bar.

- That doesn't make any sense

- What dyou – of course it – it's the work bar.

- Just because you charge your employees for a beer in the same building in which they work and then encourage them to return to their jobs does not make it a Real Thing – I won't work on Mondays anymore.

- Do you want a swimming pool – is that it?

- No.

- Because you can – you can have it all

- I don't know what that means

- All of it. You can have everything

  We can organise Spa days. Spa days can be on Wednesdays and we'll do more face masks and more pampering and we'll get faster, tougher, bigger fucking treadmills to make your body tighter and make your body softer and we'll have More chocolate and More wine and we'll have more fun and be more focused than you've ever been. Right here. Okay.

- No. Thank you.

- Would you like a work handbag?

–   No.

–   They can cost £2000, we can make that an option, we can
     make that part of your pay packet

–   No. Thank you.

–   Do you want a pay rise? Is that it? Do you want to be paid as
     much as

     as the

*Perhaps it's not clear whether the actor has forgotten their line or
it is the character tripping over a word.*

     as the

     the – sorry – as the boys?

     .

     Stop smiling.

–   (*Again, is this character or actor?*) I'm Contracted to smile

–   Not in meetings, you aren't Contracted to smile in meetings
     – Stop Smiling

–   You stop smiling.

–   I'm serious. Stop Smiling.

–   This is just my face – I Want to smile at the moment, you can't
     tell me what to do with my face

–   Whilst you're in here I Own your face

–   No you don't

–   Yes I do

–   No you don't own my face

–   I do

It feels like the actors aren't sticking to the lines, perhaps.

Okay fine I don't Own your face but I do Object to, I don't like you smiling like that whilst you're being so obtuse, I'm saying that you can bring your dogs into the work bar

— And I'm saying I refuse to recognise that as a real or legitimate space

— You Signed the petition Asking for the vending machines

— I don't want to work on Mondays

— You Signed it

— Then that was a mistake. And I apologise.

— I don't accept your apology

— That is your right

— The Problem is – and this is the Problem – the Problem is is that I don't understand

— I want Mondays off.

— Do you feel you'll be more productive?

— That's not my motivation.

— Is it about protest?

— It's about sleep.

— Because you've already got so much – is the thing – you already have so much

— It's just one day.

— Let me pour you a a a a a drink

— I don't want a drink

— Have a chocolate bar

— I don't want a chocolate bar

— Everyone Wants a ch ch ch – ch.

a Chocolate bar

–   I don't.

–   But it makes women happy.

–   I'll see you on Tuesday.

–   .

Revolutionize the Body (Make it Sexually Available. Constantly).

There are at least three people in this scene.

–   I don't understand

–   I'm not sure either of us Fully understands

–   No

–   It's – we'd really like to

–   We'd absolutely like to

–   I'd Love to understand – I'd Love to know where your head is at, what your your Thought process was

–   What led you

–   Absolutely, what Led you

–   Or – or, if I can just butt / in

–   / Please / do

–   / Perhaps Who led you, even, if I could be so so Bold

–   Quite

–   Because if Someone Else has led you

–   Well then that would be Concerning

–   Indeed

–   That would suggest

– Suggest

– That this was part of a wider problem as opposed to

– As opposed to

– A One Off.

– Because it's been a shock

– A Big shock

– For all of us

– We've never – sorry – I am so sorry – I am Talking For you

– You are

– I'm just Talking For you without checking in with

– It's fine

– Would you listen to me Talking For You – isn't that hilarious

– I feel fine about

– Because I think I Can say for both of us

– Absolutely

– When I say that we have never seen anything like it

– No

– Never

– Not once

– And – and I'm going to speak for you again

– I'm entirely happy for you to do so – we're a / team

– / A team, we are – I've interrupted you though, interrupting isn't very

– It's fine

– Team-like, but I suppose my point is

– Our point is

—   Precisely, Our Point is what the Fuck you thought you were doing.

    .

—   Or.

—   Not or. Not really Or, there isn't really an Or

—   Well

—   No Or about it

—   I suppose not

—   Because I think we'd all really like to know – myself and yourself

—   Yes

—   And the entire team really, not to mention our customers

—   Yes – the Customers, the Customers are who I'm really concerned about

—   Well, quite

—   Because we're getting complaints

—   Hundreds of complaints

—   Tens of complaints

—   Several complaints

—   And the reaction

—   On on Social media

—   Yes

—   On social media has already been Flooding in

—   Storming in

—   And the response really, from all corners has been: What the Fuck did she think she was doing – has anyone offered you a glass of water?

–   .

No.

–   That's terribly rude

–   of us – I apologise

–   Because I am aware – Fully aware

–   Completely aware

–   Aware – do you know what I'm going to say

–   well

–   One Mind – we're like One Mind

–   We're a team

–   The Engine Room

–   We're Aware, okay

–   Very Aware

–   We're So Aware

–   That

–   That

–   You're our customer too

–   One mind.

–   And it's really important – really crucially important – that We Understand our customers

–   Essential

–   It's how the company operates

–   It's on our branding

–   It's in our fucking logo – I have to apologise for my language – I do

–   It's because we feel strongly

–   We feel very passionate

–   We do

–   So – again – we'd really, really, really love to know

–   What the fuck you thought you were doing

–   What the fuck you thought you were doing lying in the middle
     of Aisle Seven with your dress over your head.

     .

–   You will have to pay for those melons.

     We literally cannot resell those melons.

–   And we want you to Have those melons

–   Of course

–   The point is, we're Happy you chose our store as the place in
     which you wish to Buy those melons

–   We fly those melons in from all sorts of countries so that you
     can just Have them

–   Without having to think about where they came from

–   That's a thing we're really proud of

–   That's a choice we're really happy you can freely make

–   We made the label 'these watermelons come from Florida via
     Guatemala and back' really very small indeed, just so that you
     don't have to feel guilty

–   Guilt-free shopping is particularly important to us

–   We want you to have it all and not feel guilty

–   Because you Absolutely can

–   But we're Concerned about

–   Yes what we're really concerned about is

— Why you chose our supermarket as the place in which to lie down and expose yourself

— There is Watermelon All Over Aisle Seven

— Which is Hazardous

— Which puts Our customers at risk

— Do you see?

— And your choice to lie down and reveal your body

— Your Breasts were fully on show

— That Choice that You made to Lie down

— Not to mention your stomach and your ribs

— That choice that you made had an impact on our Other patrons in that moment

— Because no one Asked to see that

— No one Wanted to see your flesh in Aisle Seven

— People go to Aisle Seven to buy their dairy products

— To select their yoghurts and their milk, their cheese and their cream

— Not to see your folds of skin

— And Certainly not to see your hand upon your knickers

— Or your little sausage legs wide open surrounded by cereal boxes and potatoes

— Or you Pulling your knickers down, in fact

— Or your flab. Quite frankly. Your curdled flab. The physical evidence of your regret at consuming presumably an entire Wheel of Cheese every night since you were eleven was not what our unwitting shoppers had selected to see when they rolled into Aisle Seven to select their fat-free cottage cheese.

–   So you see

–   No one wanted to see your bingo wings

–   What we're dying to know

–   Or your muffin top

–   What we

–   Or your pork belly

–   So

(*Perhaps it's not clear whether the actors have forgotten their lines at this point, or it is the characters tripping over a word.*) So. So Um to

–   Or your fucking chicken thighs you fucking chicken thighs your horrible fucking chicken thighs – I

I

–   Don't laugh

–   Not laughing not laughing.

.

I apologise.

.

–   I have felt very tired lately.

I could fall asleep standing straight up.

I'm sorry about the watermelon.

I'm not sorry about the watermelon.

.

Where my body stops and the air around it starts has felt a little like this long continuous line of a battleground for about my whole life, I think.

Fortify.

I have cut my eyelashes off. I have covered myself in coal and mud. I have bandaged my body up and made myself a collection of straight edges. Fortify. I have rubbed iodine, bleach and the gut of a rabbit into my skin until it began to burn. I have nearly emptied my body of its organs. I stopped eating for one year and three days, my body a bouquet of shell bone. I have eaten only animal fat until I rolled, bubbled and whaled and came quite close to popping. Fortify. Make my edges clear. Where I begin and air stops is my motherland. No? I have sat under sun lamps until my skin crackled, spat and blistered. I have pulled my hair out with my fingers and my teeth out with pliers. I have wrapped myself in clingfilm, foil, clothes, make-up and barbed wire.

No fortification strong enough.

Nothing to stop them wanting to come in.

Lie down.

Lie down and become available. Constantly. Want to be entered. Constantly. It cannot be an Invasion, if you want it. They Cannot Invade if you Want It. Open your legs and throw your dress over your head, pull your knickers down and want it and they can invade you no longer.

Get wet.

Get wet.

Get wetter.

Turn on. Turn on. Turn on.

And want it. And want it. Constantly. Constantly. Constantly want it. Remove the edges of your body. Choose. My body is no battleground, there is no longer a line of defense – I Am Open. There are borders here no more. This body this land is unattackable, unprotected, unconquerable, unclaimable, no different from air around it or bodies coming in because there Is no in to come into, you cannot overpower it because

I have given it you cannot rape it because I choose it you
cannot take because I give it and because I choose it
I choose it I choose it

Constantly.

This World Can Never Attack Me Again.

Because I Choose it. Over and Again and Again and Over.

.

—   I.

—   (*Is this the character or the actor?*) I'm sorry. I'm not sure
what happens now?

—   .

Act Two

Revolutionize the World (Don't Reproduce).

This Act is continuous. The titles do not break the action.

A farm. **Dinah** *holds* **Agnes**'s *hand. It doesn't matter if* **Grandma** *looks very young.*

Dinah   I don't sleep anymore.

Do you?

.

Hello.

I wanted to tell you that I understood. That I had reached a place of total acceptance that I had developed the kind of understanding that rooted deep, deep enough to not care about what the outcome of this conversation might be.

But of course that isn't the case.

.

Do I look at all different then?

.

Grandma   You're a little taller probably.

I don't have much skill for remembering faces.

Dinah   Nothing about my eyes or my smile?

Grandma   Haven't seen you smile. Couldn't comment.

Dinah   I'm finding it hard to.

It's like smog. Or water. It's not as light as it used to be – Air, I'm talking about the Air, I.

It's physically impossible. Sleeping.

I'm beyond feeling it now.

.

The plan was to get in the car and drive for three days
– which we did – to bring you bread and jam – which
we did – to pick you flowers – which we did – and to
stand in front of you and tell you that I understand.
That I completely understand. And that I forgive you.
And then we would drive home but we would stop at
the end of the first day, not Drive continuously as we
did on our way here, but stop and pull in somewhere
by a little wood and sleep.

.

But I don't understand.

And this morning, there was a line across the sky, a
completely legible black line that seemed to mark the
journey back, away from you and the temptation to
take that was enormous because I know you probably
won't help me you probably don't give a and there is
something about all of this that I can Bear I can
shoulder I can do, but Agnes – Agnes's mouth bleeds,
she scratches and she scratches at it until it bleeds and
she has started to stop talking, she won't eat, she
won't lift her hands, she can't keep hold of a thing,
not a thing, she is starting to disappear entirely and
and and I think if you can tell her she came from
somewhere good then it might stop.

.

Grandma   Agnes?

Dinah   .

This is Agnes.

She gave you the bluebells

Grandma	She dropped the bluebells
Dinah	She's tired. She can't hold any – she's tired.
Grandma	Everybody's tired all of a sudden
Dinah	(*Is this the actor or the character?*) This is Hard – this is really getting Harder I

I feel. I'm. Sorry.

Okay.

.

This looks wonderful. Really. Really. Is it all home grown?

Grandma	I grew it. If that's what you mean. Or I killed it.

If that's what you mean.

Dinah	It's so impressive.

What an achievement.

It's really remarkable, it's.

.

This is Agnes. Your Granddaughter. Agnes.

Grandma	.

Shall we eat.

Dinah	Your granddaughter. Agnes.
Grandma	That'll be impossible, Dinah.
Dinah	Your granddaughter. Agnes.
Grandma	I have no granddaughter.
Dinah	Your flesh and blood. Your granddaughter. Agnes.
Grandma	My flesh and my blood are all contained within my body.

Dinah   Agnes was born of my body, I was born of your body.

Grandma   You're your own body.

Dinah   I don't understand, I'm your child

Grandma   I have no children.

                    I had no children.

Revolutionize the Work (Don't Do It).

                    Serve the potatoes then Agnes.

Agnes *looks*.

Dinah   I

Grandma   There's butter over there, and there's wine on that shelf.

                    Pour it.

Dinah   She doesn't

Grandma   She can pour some wine. Her hands aren't bleeding.
                    She has all her fingers.

Dinah   She's your granddaughter.

Grandma   There's meat. She can carve it.

Dinah   This is the first time I have sat with my family around
                    me and

Grandma   I'm not your family, Dinah.

                    .

Dinah   Will we say Grace?

Grandma   Cut some of that bread.

Dinah   We should say Grace

Grandma   Can say what the fuck you like.

Dinah   We always used to say Grace

Grandma   Put salt on the potatoes.

Dinah   Such Excitement when it was My turn to say Grace

Grandma   You can get that cheese from the side there.

Dinah   Sitting at the Big table giving thanks for watermelons
– I Always gave thanks for watermelons

Grandma   You. Say Grace then /

/ **Agnes** *sings. It hurts. She stops.*

Revolutionize the Language (That Word Doesn't Exist Here).

Grandma   I said Grace. That wasn't Grace.

Agnes   Grayce. Grayssss. Grace. ssssss. I

Dinah   It was beautiful, it was like a

Agnes   Buuuuuutifull I don't

Dinah   Little nightingale, it was lovely and and perfect and

Agnes   Luv luvvvv luvl I I'm sorry I don't [understand]

Dinah   She

Grandma   I said Grace not

Dinah   Be kind. Be kind, please. Be kind.

Agnes   Kynd. Kiiiind. Kind. Kind. I don't. I'm sorry. I don't
understand. I. I. (*Is this the actor's confusion, or the
character?*) I'm sorry, I really don't understand.

Dinah   You don't have to under[stand] – she doesn't have to
[understand] – it gets harder and harder and

Revolutionize the World (Don't Associate with Men)

A man enters.

Grandma   Get out

The man leaves.

Revolutionize the Body (Stop Eating).

Grandma   Will she not eat?

Dinah   Please don't ask that.

Revolutionize the Body / The Language (Stop Speaking).

Grandma   Do you want something?

Agnes   .

Grandma   What does she want?

Agnes *smiles.*

Revolutionize the Body (Start to Shut it Down).

Grandma   Her mouth is bleeding.

Dinah   You got trapped. You were completely trapped.
                Daddy beat you up. He kicked the living shit out of you.

                My Daddy – that man you lived with and had sex with
                and children were then produced – He used to Jump.
                With Boots on.

                Upon your neck.

                He used to hold a lit match between your legs and if
                you flinched he would punch upwards, breaking the
                walls of your cunt.

                He used to bite your breasts until they bled. He used
                to kick your knees for hours, not particularly hard, not

his hardest, but kick until his back was drenched in
sweat and your bones were shattered.

He used to rape you, he used to –

(*Is this the character or the actor?*) Sorry – sorry –
am I Sexualising all this a bit too um. Am I making
this Sexy – he used to, okay, okay okay okay okay,
my Daddy used to beat the crap out of you and you
had to get out, you had to get out and forget you had
children, forget it all and begin again, I can
understand that

Agnes *retches.*

Grandma Not what happened.

That didn't happen, none of that happened.

Dinah My father was the kindest man – I'm trying to – so
you felt you'd gotten very ill. You'd fallen very
terribly gravely ill – can I smoke

Grandma Can do what the fuck you like

Dinah You were diseased, riddled with it, getting weaker by
the day and you had to retreat you had to go away
rather than know your family had to watch you suffer,
forget it all, forget it all forget all the children and
begin again, I can understand that. Though of course
you should be dead.

Grandma Never been ill a day in my life.

Dinah You were depressed. Contemplating suicide.

It was too awful to imagine that And have children.

Grandma Not so.

Agnes *vomits.*

Dinah (*Is this the character or the actor??*) That is
Disgusting – I am just Trying – trying to get an insight
into, some understanding of, because it seems I came

from nowhere kind, nowhere kind and I haven't been
able to give anything good to my girl, not one good
thing and now – was it the environment – did you feel
a sudden jolt, a sudden panic that you had offloaded
such a Dent into the world, a whole new carbon
footprint, a new person to help deplete the fish stocks
and pollute the skies and get on planes on planes on
planes and contribute to the rise of the sea, was that
why you left me on my fourth birthday and decided to
renounce your children – more than that – deny you'd
ever birthed them in the first place – the others are all
Dead by the way so my breathing, my being here feels
miraculous – did you do it for love of the planet

Grandma   No

Dinah   For the love of a man

Grandma   No

Dinah   For the love of a woman

Grandma   No

Dinah   Say you did for the love of something, for one good
thing, one good reason, she's splitting into the
smallest pieces, she has never known goodness

Grandma   There isn't much goodness.

Dinah   Was it that I waged a little war upon your body?

Was it that I ruined smooth lines – was it that
everyone says it's the most natural thing a woman
Can possibly do but it's havoc and perhaps I shattered
your hips in the process and shit is everywhere,
suddenly shit is everywhere, was it that?

Was it because I was a girl?

If I had had a dick you could have chopped it off in
protest, I could have been political – was it that?

Did I break your heart?

Did I ruin your life?

Did I make you incapable of love – did you hold a thing so big and so fucking precious near your ribs and then in I came and destroyed it, in I came – or out I came – splitting your body in two and someone put me up at your breast up near your heart and where there had been promise and love and hope there was fucking pus?

Tell her.

Tell her.

Tell her so she can know goodness. Tell me so I can sleep – (*Is this the character or the actor??!*) I am so so very tired I don't know what to do.

.

Grandma and **Agnes** *pick up their knives and forks. They chop their tongues out.*

Act Three

Galvanise

The line between actor and character can be paper thin here. At some point, the actors will have to be in more than one scene at the same time. It is okay to find that difficult.

– OH MY GOD I'VE ABSOLUTELY FUCKING CRACKED IT.

.

– I am never aroused by porn. I am never aroused by porn. I am never aroused by porn. Porn. Never. Arouses me.

– I REFUSE TO BAKE THE FOLLOWING	– Naaaaaaailed it!
.	Sorry.
.	
THE FOLLOWING ITEMS. I REFUSE TO BAKE CUPCAKES. I PARTICULARLY REFUSE TO BAKE HEART-SHAPED GOODS. I DO NOT SELL GLITTER.	

Please click on About
Me for more info

and feedback.

–

I Will close my eyes if I
see a pornographic

picture and yes, I will be
compiling a petition. In
Relation. To it.
And a survey. And yes,
yes, I probably will run
for parliament.
Thank you.
Thank you so much.

– Does this pass the
Bechdel test?

– No. No, I don't
think so.

–

Hymens! Unruptured
hymens for sale.
Perfectly intact.
Hymens! Come and
buy our hymens –
carefully removed,
perfectly intact,
utterly unravished!

– Because. Okay. Because. And this is exciting, this is
really the Nuts but –
Shit.

Leaves.

– What're you doing?

– (*Is this the actor or the character?*) Ummmm.

– What're you Doing?

– None of your beeswax

– Think it is my beeswax

– Just 'cos you're wearing A Uniform does not mean it is your beeswax.

– That is Exactly what it means

   You know you're not supposed to be down here.

– Who says?

– Law.

– This alley backs onto my house

– Right

– Not that it Is any of your beeswax, but this alley backs onto my property.

– Still can't be down here

– Why not?

– For your own safety. Not allowed in alleys.

   You know that.

– WE'VE GOT LITERALLY SO MUCH WORK TO DO!

– She is Fiercely intelligent. She can be a little bit emotional, agreed, but she is fiercely intelligent – a little on the aggressive side. But she's fearless too. Fearless. And occasionally manipulative. She's a really vital member of the team. She's adjectives. And. (*Perhaps it's not clear whether the actor has forgotten their line, or it is the character tripping over a word.*) She's lots of adjectives and describing words.

   Him? He's great.

– Because. Okay.
   Because. And this is

exciting. It is it is it is.
Just need a second to.
Catch my.
But I've been
thinking. I've been
taking Time and Space
to Think very deeply
and I've got this feeling
all the way down to my
bones, to my marrow,
that that okay, that –
and this is fucking It

– I'm not really sure I get your point.

That.
Um. That.
thinking
that.

.

– He seems very Unhappy
– That's not unusual
– He cries. All of the time.
– He's a child.
– He drew this picture yesterday.
– Okay.

– I HAVE GOT LITERALLY NO MAKE-UP ON

Alright.
You want me to hang it on my fridge?

– That's not my – I'm just trying to figure out if there are things Going On at home that might explain some of his feelings.

– His feelings?

– He said this picture was called 'Me and My Cellulite'

	– Okay.
	– We talked about wishes yesterday. He said he wished he had a thigh gap.
	.
– I have been thinking.	– Right?
	– He had one piece of watermelon in his lunchbox today.
	He says he's fat. He says he's disgustingly fat.
– 'Scuse me? Ummm	– He is. Isn't he? They're all fat. Aren't they?
You're supposed to OI. OI. OI	– He's four.
	– Okay – What're you Doing?
	.

–   Me?

–   Yeah you – What're you Doing?

–   I'm making T-shirts. And pants. And pencil cases. Merch.

–   Merch?

–   Merchandise.

| –   What d'you | –   I HAVE BEEN THINKING. |

.

–   This one says NO SEXISM

–   You cannot be

–   This one says STOP BEING SEXIST. Merch.

–   You have to be kidding

–   This one says LET'S BE EQUAL YEAH?

.

She chops her head off.

– takes a big breath, ready to speak –

–   Who is that man? Mowing the lawn? His feet are
    bleeding.

–   Ummmmmm. Sorry. Hang on a. I'm not supposed to
    do this one – it's

–   Who is that man? Mowing the lawn? His feet are
    bleeding.

–   No, I'm not in

–   No – seriously. Who is that man? Mowing the lawn?
    His feet are bleeding.

–   Ohhh. Him? He raped
    that girl. The
    disabled one.
    He's doing community   –   Hymens! Still for sale!
    service   Reduced! Hymens,
                                      come and get your
                                      hymens!

–   Adverb adjective noun. Adverb adjective noun. Adverb
    adjective noun. Do you see?

–   The thing is – the Thing that I've been thinking

–   Yeah I absolutely wholeheartedly Get that, I really Do,
    it's just that it's near impossible with no evidence, d'you
    know what I mean?

–   I

–   Yeah, d'you know what I mean?

–   I'm sorry, I literally have no idea what you

With the fact of the matter of me being a police officer
that you have called here to the scene of the crime

– Oh. Yes. Right. Um. Evidence. You said something
about

Evidence

– Yes exactly, in that there is none so it's impossible to
push on in our investigations at the time being for now
unfortunately

– With the –

Okay.   –   Sorry to interrupt
Hang on a, because it's
getting impossible to Think.
I haven't got any stuff.

– Yeah no sure, absolutely, but that could of course just be a
Choice you've made in terms of your living arrangements
– you would need to prove that you Had stuff

– I'm really tired

– Sure   –   Sorry, but

– Um, the uh, my windows are all smashed

– Yeah, but again, who's to say
You didn't do that yourself

– I've got blood all over my legs

– I'm not judging   –   Sorry to

– My blood is everywhere

– Yeah, but it's just that
there's no evidence

                                          –   Sorry to interrupt

– Yeah?

– I just I wanted to

– You're fine

–   I just – I wanted to just ask if you could not do that

–   Do what

–   That thing you're about to do – be fucked in your
    arsehole by that dog whilst those men jizz on your
    face 'til you vomit and they make you eat it up again –
    could you not do that?

    .

–   Ummm. It's sort of the
    Main Action of the scene.

–   Totally appreciate
    that – really do. Bills   –   Um.
    to pay and and that.
    It's just that everyone
    thinks that's sex now.

–   Would I describe   –   Can't feel my legs
    myself as a [feminist] –.
    yeah Absolutely,
    Absolutely. I mean, as
    a Father of a girl –
    how could I not be?

–   Would I describe
    myself [as a feminist] –
    of course, of course –
    I'm married. To A
    Woman. How could
    I not be? Please!

–   Would I – I've got
    a mother haven't I?
    Think About That.

–   Naturally. I walk past
    women all the time.
    Course I am.

–   I've seen a woman
     before. Round things.
     Absolutely I support
     the round ones. 100%.

–   I'd need to See a   –   (*Throws a bucket of water*
     woman I think before   *over herself and slaps*
     I said if I was one for   *herself.*)
     sure, I'd need to know   THIS FEELS
     what it was exactly I   AMAZING
     was supporting, but   GENUINELY
     essentially, yeah, sure   INCREDIBLE. I

–   Yes. I'm a Human, so   AM HAVING A
     Yes.   WONDERFUL TIME.

–   I think I thought it was   –   THIS FEELS
     something else.   AMAZING
     SHUT THE FUCK UP.

I think. I think I thought it was something smaller than
it is. And actually. Actually it's Enormous. Actually
it's a Massive Fuck Off Explosion we're after. Because
really. Really there's nowhere else to go.

                              –   An Englishman,
                                   Irishman and a
                                   Scottishman all go into a
                                   bar

                              –   Yeah

                              –   RAPE!

There is a human in
between the two people.
speaking   *They laugh.*
                              –   That is undoubtedly
                                   funny

– I'm so sorry

– Are you okay?

– No, I'm so sorry – I feel awful, but

– What is it?

– It's just that. Well.

   You're trespassing.

– Sorry?

– On my property – you're trespassing – just. Here. See.
   Trespass – you're um. You're trespassing.

   .

– Oh God, am I really?

– Mmmm   –   Adverb adjective noun.

– I had no / idea   Adverb adjective noun.

– / Yeah, no, it's – you're   Adverb adjective noun.
   / trespassing

– / God, how embarrassing /

– / No, it's fine, it's just –
   belongs to me / so

– / I feel Awful / Totally

– / These things happen,
   it's just, you know / it

– / Absolutely – I feel /
   terrible

– No it's – not to worry.

   Need to get You a bigger
   No Trespassing sign.

   They laugh.

\-   (*Running round.*) My choice my choice

my choice my choice	–	Dearly beloved
my choice my choice	–	No
my choice my choice	–	We are gathered here
my choice my choice		today
my choice my choice	–	Absolutely fucking not
my choice my choice	–	In the Sight of
choice my choice my	–	No way Jose
choice my choice my	–	Please.
choice my choice my	–	No
choice my choice my	–	Please?
choice my choice my	–	No
choice my choice my	–	Go On
choice my choice my	–	I'm not marrying him
choice my choice my	–	Give it a go
choice my choice my	–	He raped me.
choice my choice my	–	Yeah but
choice my choice my	–	And I'm twelve
choice my choice my	–	But this is nicest for
choice my choice my		everyone
choice my choice my		
choice my choice my		
choice my choice my		
choice my choice my		
choice my choice my		
choice my choice my		
choice my choice my		
choice – it really Is Better		
and safest and Nicest		
for everyone		Yes, see Nicest for
		everyone

if You stay Indoors
because otherwise
you might get attacked
and we can all go
Outdoors but because   –   WOMAN FOR SALE!
none of You will be   WHOLE HUMAN

Outdoors then none of
Us will be able to attack
you so that's Nicest

FOR SALE! IN THE
NAME OF AHM
SOMETHING
REALLY BIG –
WOMAN FOR SALE,
ENTIRE WOMAN
FOR SALE

– Still trespassing

– Oops!

They laugh.

It's because it's So Easy
So Easy to do

– I'm not doing it
– But I'm needed over
there

– Hymens are for sale,
just at the back there by
the watermelons and
the bluebells and the
potatoes and the cup-
cakes and some canned
goods.

– I'm tired
– He's mowing the lawn
because he raped
someone
This is called Me
and My Cellulite
Why had everyone in
her family lost

– YOU CAN'T
TRESPASS HERE
I AM HOLDING
A FUCKING NO
TRESPASS SIGN
FOR A REASON
YOU ABSOLUTE
FUCKTARD.

Adjective adverb noun.
Adjective adverb
noun. And so on.

My choice my choice
my choice
.
Absolutely.

– Brilliant

– Isn't it? I am having
THE BEST TIME

– Not possible because
   I am / HAVING THE
   BEST TIME

– / THE BEST TIME

– Could you shut up?

– Porn is not arousing –   – My choice my choice
   porn never ever   my choice
   ever arousing   .

– Except when it is horse   And then you're
                                supposed to say . . .

porn.   .

Obviously.

– Well. Obviously. – And then it's   – Aren't you a
   Obviously when   your line.   bit exhausted?
   it is horse porn   I Say. My choice   Hasn't the blood
   then that is a   my choice my   drained from
   different matter.   choice . . .   you?
   Obviously that   And then you   .
   is entirely   say . . .   Don't you feel a
   arousing.   .   little like
– Dolphins rape   you've lost any
   other dolphins   My choice my   grasp on life you
   of course.   choice my   had – don't you
                       choice.

– Of course
– It happens in
the natural
world all the
time which is
probably why
humans do it –

because nature
does it first and
I don't think it's
that we're
anthropo-
morphising
their behaviour
to justify our
behaviour – I
don't think it's
that at all
– No not at all –
do you know
your lines?
– No, not a single
one I've been
making the
whole thing up
– The whole thing?
– Literally made
up every single
one of these
words

Hymens

.

Aaaaand
Fat little boys

and stuff.

And
merchandise
and alleys
and threesomes
and make-up
and stuff and
and and and
and and
so on and so
forth and so on
and adjectives
and describing
words and more
describing
words and
then some more
describing
words and more
describing words

feel like you've lost
all sense of what life
is supposed to be?

.

Don't you feel
like it's drifted
away from you?
The point of it
all?
And isn't having
that thought
utterly
exhausting and.
More than that
More than that
really
Definitely more
than that
Actually,
definitively with
the could you
just SHUT THE
FUCK UP?

– There is a point at which the thought is not enough.
The thought can be in my head the thought can exist
up here in my head or wherever we carry thoughts
perhaps, perhaps it is closer to my heart or my guts
or somewhere in my intestines but the thought can

be the thing, the beautiful perfect thing, the thought
can be the Entire World for as long as you are happy
for it to just be the thought and it is like a needle, it
is like a needle has pushed in on my skin and settled
somewhere in my system, big and perfect and whole
but unfinished because you need it to finish you need
it to end and aren't you tired aren't you exhausted
aren't you livid and famished and desperate now
because the thought the thought that seemed simple
is not enough and I think we fucked it up I think we
made a mistake somewhere along the way which is
ludicrous which is desperately desperately desperate
because I think I have been living on the principle of
kindness and hope being enough and the thought being
enough but it turns out it isn't it turns out we stopped
watching and checking and nurturing the thought to
become the action at some point because at some
point I opened my eyes at some point I looked up and
it felt like wastelands and wastelands and wastelands
and wastelands had grown where we thought we were
building mountains because now I stand where I
thought there would be rolling rolling mountains and it
is a little patch of dirt where potatoes and bluebells and
watermelons wouldn't deign to grow let alone progress
let alone a thing like progress because your choice your
choice your choice and my choice have turned out to
be not the fertile soil we thought we were standing two
feet apart upon but dry and arid and empty and alone
because the thought the thought the thought hasn't
been enough hasn't been the thing hasn't been –

Loud noise. It is cold. It is bright. And then it is black.

Act Four

This scene should be between four women.

– I feel ready.

– Are you sure

– I feel completely ready. It feels like an inevitability.

.

– It may take years.

– It probably will.

– Imagine if it took weeks

– Or just one day

– Wouldn't that be fucking

– We're going to dismantle the monetary system

– Yes

– And overthrow the government

– Yes

– We'll expect other countries to follow suit

– Yes

– Quickly, and we have plans in place for that

– Of course

– All jobs will be destroyed

– And all couples broken

– And we take over the airwaves, the televisions, the Internet, etcetera.

.

—   And we'll eradicate all men.

.

—   Yes.

.

—   As a necessity.

—   Yes.

.

—   You sound sad

—   I am sad

—   It won't work if you're sad

—   It won't work if you aren't.

It failed. The whole world failed at it. It could have been so brilliant. How strange of you not to feel sad.

Who knew that life could be so awful.

.

Notes

11   *North Korea*: officially the Democratic People's Republic of Korea which occupies the northern part of the Korean peninsula.
Governed by an oppressive regime, the country is isolated from the international community and is often criticized for its human rights violations and its nuclear weapons which pose a global threat.

18   *Spanner*: also a wrench. A metal tool with a shaped end used to turn objects.

18   *Chomping down upon you*: biting with force.

21   *Liberalism*: an ideology based on an understanding of the rights and freedom of the individual. It is often used to suggest an empathy with different points of view.

22   *I feel Concerned About where diamonds come from*: the mining of diamonds has been called out for its exploitation of child labour, the contamination of land and water and the displacement of indigenous populations.

25   *Chattel*: an item of property. It also refers to the human body as property in the context of slavery and the slave-trade (e.g. chattel slavery).

32   *Do you want to be paid as much as [. . .] the boys?*: despite many reforms to improve equal pay between the sexes, the gender pay gap still affects a large proportion of the female workforce.

38   *We made the label 'these watermelons come via Florida and Guatemala and back' really very small indeed, just so you don't have to feel guilty*: the transport of goods from different parts of the world produces a significant proportion of carbon emissions thus contributing to climate change.

40   *Bingo wings*: a sexist and ageist expression that refers to the folds of skin in the arm of a woman who plays Bingo, a game popular among older women. Part of the game includes shouting 'Bingo' by raising your arm when you win.

40   *Muffin top*: another sexist expression denoting the body fat across a person's waistline.

53   *Bechdel test*: the act of measuring gender equality in a work of art (e.g. film, book, play). It takes its name from the American cartoonist Alison Bechdel whose 1985 comic strip 'The Rule' features a female character who claims she will only watch films that have at least two women discussing a subject other than men.

53   *petition*: a written request signed by several people appealing to a
      higher authority with the aim to reverse a social injustice.
53   *Hymens*: a hymen is a thin membrane at the entrance of a girl's
      vagina signifying her virginity. In ancient Greek mythology, Hymen
      was the God of marriage. In some cultures, if women lose their
      virginity before marriage they are considered impure and cannot get
      married.
54   *None of your beeswax*: slang for 'none of your business'.